Strategic Studies Institute
and
U.S. Army War College Press

STRATEGIC IMPLICATIONS OF THE EVOLVING SHANGHAI COOPERATION ORGANIZATION

Henry Plater-Zyberk
with
Andrew Monaghan

August 2014

*****

*****

Comments pertaining to this report are invited and should be forwarded to: Director, Strategic Studies Institute and U.S. Army War College Press, U.S. Army War College, 47 Ashburn Drive, Carlisle, PA 17013-5010.

*****

This manuscript was funded by the U.S. Army War College External Research Associates Program. Information on this program is available on our website, *www.StrategicStudies Institute.army.mil*, at the Opportunities tab.

*****

*****

The Strategic Studies Institute and U.S. Army War College Press publishes a monthly email newsletter to update the national security community on the research of our analysts, recent and forthcoming publications, and upcoming conferences sponsored by the Institute. Each newsletter also provides a strategic commentary by one of our research analysts. If you are interested in receiving this newsletter, please subscribe on the SSI website at *www.StrategicStudiesInstitute.army.mil/newsletter*.

FOREWORD

The role of the Shanghai Cooperation Organization (SCO) in regional politics, and the significance of the organization for U.S. interests, is widely misunderstood. The organization is emphatically not a military bloc, and yet engages in joint activities which resemble military cooperation to U.S. eyes. It is, in theory, open to new members; but at present is highly unlikely to accept any. Its rhetoric firmly opposes U.S. presence and activity on the territory of member states, and yet individual member states leverage basing agreements with the United States to their advantage.

This monograph by Mr. Henry Plater-Zyberk seeks to explain the SCO through reviewing its history and stated aspirations, and measuring these against actual achievements. It concludes that with the notable exception of the Regional Anti-Terrorist Structure (RATS), the great majority of SCO accomplishments are of little significance other than to provide an additional multinational vehicle through which China, and in particular Russia, can seek to counter U.S. and Western activity in Central Asia.

Specific policy aims of the SCO, (or of Russia or China through the medium of the SCO), should not be analyzed according to U.S. policy criteria. It is not necessary for an event to take place that would be considered by the United States as a substantial policy achievement, in order for Russia to believe that the SCO has contributed to countering U.S. aims as part of an overall strategy. The Strategic Studies Institute therefore recommends this monograph as a key to understanding the real implications of development of the SCO for U.S. interests, and where and how these should be resisted.

Douglas C. Lovelace

DOUGLAS C. LOVELACE, JR.
Director
Strategic Studies Institute and
    U.S. Army War College Press

ABOUT THE AUTHORS

HENRY PLATER-ZYBERK joined the United Kingdom (UK) Ministry of Defence's Conflict Studies Research Centre (CSRC) as a senior lecturer/analyst. His previous service with the Royal Air Force Reserve was in a variety of roles making use of his extensive language skills. During his career with CSRC, Mr. Plater-Zyberk wrote and briefed prolifically on political and internal security issues of Russia and other former Soviet states, regularly lecturing to the staff colleges and defense establishments of the UK and other North Atlantic Treaty Organization (NATO) nations. Between assignments, he maintained his language skills and close contact with the targets of his research by assisting bilateral negotiations and direct military-to-military exchanges as a facilitator and multilingual interpreter. When writing on particularly sensitive topics, Mr. Plater-Zyberk also published under the pseudonym Gordon Bennett. He retired from full-time research in 2011, and now serves as a Senior Research Fellow at the Prague Security Studies Institute, while working on a comprehensive history of the Soviet and post-Soviet security and intelligence services. Mr. Plater-Zyberk holds a degree in Russian from the University of London.

ANDREW MONAGHAN is a Research Fellow in the Russia and Eurasia Programme at Chatham House and Academic Visitor at St. Antony's College, Oxford, UK. Additionally, he is the Founder and Director of the Russia Research Network, an independent organization for the generation of information and expertise on Russian politics, security, and economic issues based in London. In this capacity, he has served as an expert witness to the House of Commons Foreign Affairs Select Committee. Until late-2012, Dr. Monaghan directed Russia related research in the Research Division of the NATO Defense College (NDC) in Rome. In this role, he was also the NDC's senior researcher on energy security matters. Prior to that, he held positions as a Senior Research Associate at the Advanced Research and Assessment Group (ARAG), part of the Defence Academy of the UK, and a Visiting Lecturer in the Defence Studies Department of King's College, London, the civilian academic arm of the Joint Services Command and Staff College at the Defence Academy. Dr. Monaghan holds an M.A. in war studies and a Ph.D. in Russian foreign policy (Russian perspectives of Russia-European Union security relations) from the Department of War Studies, King's College, UK.

SUMMARY

Key points from this analysis include:
- The Shanghai Cooperation Organization (SCO) is an enduring association which was originally brought together by the short-term border security interests of its first five members.
- Russia believes it plays a leading role in the SCO; in fact, however, the organization is and always has been driven by China, and Moscow's role is vital but secondary. The other member states, former Central Asian Soviet republics with no history of modern statehood or governance, are not equal partners—but their geostrategic location and, in some cases, natural resources make them potentially valuable allies for the United States and other major powers.
- The SCO is unlikely to enlarge further. Since its inception, the SCO has received several applications for membership. However, any enlargement of the organization could be fraught with difficulties, mainly because of conflicts of interest between China and Russia and the fear by member states that some new candidates are potential international liabilities and may create further conflict within the organization.
- SCO's most important and best-functioning component structure to date has been its Regional Anti-Terrorist Structure (RATS).[1] Following the U.S. and North Atlantic Treaty Organization drawdown in Afghanistan in 2014, the RATS will certainly be reinforced, but there is no indication to date that the organization as a whole will move any closer to becoming a military alliance.

- Recent announcements that the SCO will improve its multidirectional cooperation do not seem to be supported by specific planning or political determination. Only unforeseen and extraordinary world events could make the SCO member states move closer towards real political, economic, or military integration, with all the long-term strategic implications that would entail.
- While the SCO as an organization does not mount any direct challenge to U.S. interests, its political role as a coalition of anti-U.S. sentiment is likely to develop further in the future.
- Bilateral security cooperation with the Central Asian members of the SCO is ripe for development, but this will require careful and tactful management of their balance of interests between the United States, China, and Russia.

ENDNOTES - SUMMARY

1. The SCO Regional Anti-Terrorist Structure is sometimes translated, especially by Chinese sources, as the Regional Counter-Terrorist Structure (RCTS).

STRATEGIC IMPLICATIONS OF THE EVOLVING SHANGHAI COOPERATION ORGANIZATION

AN ACCIDENTAL ALLIANCE

Looking closely at the early development of the Shanghai Cooperation Organization (SCO) shows us two things: first, the consistent leading role taken by China from the earliest stages; and second, the manner in which the organization in its current form developed almost by accident from a series of short-term measures intended to resolve border security issues.

China reacted almost instantly to the dissolution of the Union of Soviet Socialist Republics (USSR) at the end of 1991. While the political situation in Russia was still close to chaos with a consequent near paralysis of foreign policy, China did not suffer from the same problems and moved rapidly to investigate the opportunities presented by the newly independent states in its vicinity. At the very beginning of January 1992, a Chinese government delegation led by Minister of Foreign Trade Li Lanqing was already on a whistle-stop political reconnaissance tour of all five former Soviet Central Asian republics.[1] This started an intensive round of bilateral visits and agreement signing between Central Asian states and China during the rest of 1992,[2] which laid the groundwork for a new order of cooperative relations in the region.

The main initial driver for security cooperation between the current members of the SCO was resolving border demarcation issues. This was significant when considering Chinese relations with Russia, Kazakhstan, Kyrgyzstan, and Tajikistan, all of which had disputed borders with China as a consequence of the Soviet period. China's borders with the new states were about 3,700 kilometers long, and as well as demarcation, Beijing was also concerned about the freedom of movement across the old Soviet borders of increasingly aggressive Islamic groups, and their potential influence on China's own Uighur minority in Xinjiang.

On September 8, 1992, at a meeting in Minsk, the countries of Belarus, Russia, Kazakhstan, Kyrgyzstan, and Tajikistan agreed on a common border policy with China. The four former republics of the Soviet Union also agreed to send a joint delegation to have border talks with Beijing, China. When the talks began, the three Central Asian countries had a total of 19 disputed border areas with China (11 between China and Kazakhstan, five between Kyrgyzstan and China, and three between Tajikistan and China).[3] China's border differences with Kazakhstan and Kyrgyzstan were solved with a mutually acceptable agreement at the end of 1999, and with Tajikistan in May 2002,[4] and China and Russia signed the final border agreement on October 14, 2004.[5] An additional agreement—finalizing the completion of the 4,300-km border demarcation—was signed by the foreign ministers of both countries on July 21, 2008.[6]

Yet even at an early stage of the long negotiations on border issues, shared security concerns were leading to additional closer cooperation over and above demarcation. Recognition of the unique challenges of the time led to unprecedented multilateral cooperative security initiatives. Five countries (Russia, Kazakhstan, Kyrgyzstan, Tajikistan, and China) started parallel, independent talks on reduction of their armed forces and confidence building measures in the border areas of the countries concerned. The "Shanghai Five" group was officially established on April 26, 1996, with the signing in Shanghai of the "Agreement on Strengthening of Confidence Building Measures in the Military Sphere in Border Regions." The second meeting of the new organization took place in Moscow, where on April 24, 1997, the "four plus one" countries agreed to reduce military forces in these border areas.[7]

Meanwhile, cultivation by China of Central Asian states on a bilateral basis continued. In April 1994, Chinese Prime Minister Li Peng visited Uzbekistan, Turkmenistan, Kazakhstan, and Kyrgyzstan.[8] During his visit, Li stated four principles of the developing relationship between China and Central Asia. All of these principles contain phrases which are familiar from habitual Chinese discourse, with underlying meanings which are strikingly different from general principles of foreign relations followed by the United States:

1. Maintaining good neighborly, friendly, peaceful coexistence.

2. Developing mutually beneficial cooperation which would contribute to the overall prosperity of the region.

3. Respecting the decisions taken by each nation, and noninterference with the policies of other states.

4. Respect for the independence and sovereignty of each country and a promotion of regional stability.[9]

Jiang Zemin, China's then President and General Secretary of the Central Committee of the Communist Party of China, was next to visit in July 1996 and also visited Uzbekistan, Kyrgyzstan, and Kazakhstan. In his speech in Almaty, Kazakhstan, on July 5, 1996, Jiang stressed the importance of long-term, stable relations between China and its neighbors.[10]

The next meeting of the Shanghai Five in Almaty on July 3-4, 1998, saw for the first time five separate delegations representing their national interests. The Shanghai Five issued "The Almaty Declaration," in which they expressed a desire to continue security cooperation and an intention to widen their activities in Central Asia and across the whole continent.[11] The signatories of the declaration criticized any form of nationalist separatism and religious extremism. They agreed to cooperate on combating terrorism, organized crime, weapons and drugs trafficking, and other illegal activities in the region, and declared their willingness to widen cooperation to energy, transport, and other economic issues. Finally, the five states expressed their concern about the situation in Afghanistan.

The Almaty meeting was the turning point when the Shanghai Five changed from a confidence-building organization primarily preoccupied with border issues and hard security, into a multidirectional organization with considerably broader potential. At this point, Russia, then led by Boris Yeltsin, was still economically weak, indecisive, and unstable, and served as a warning for the former Soviet republics rather than an example to emulate. Had Moscow been more determined, able, and willing to invest money and political effort to build up the Shanghai Five, the organization would probably now be called the Almaty Cooperation Organization and dominated by Russia. However, with their booming economy, effective centralized decisionmaking and clear foreign policy objectives, China gradually took the initiative to lead the group into a new alliance. The Shanghai Five met next in August 1999 in Bishkek, Kyrgyzstan, at the height of the Kyrgyz–Uzbek conflict in the Batken area. At this meeting, the Kyrgyz delegation proposed establishing a Regional Anti-Terrorist Structure (RATS) based in Bishkek. In December 1999, also in Bishkek, the Shanghai Five held their first joint meeting of state security and law enforcement officials.[12]

Uzbekistan was seen by all five countries as an important partner, conducting a consistent campaign against Islamic radicals on its own territory and also bordering all four remaining Central Asian countries and Afghanistan. Yet, it was not until the Shanghai Five Summit in Dushanbe, Tajikistan, in the summer of 2000, that a meeting of the Five was attended by President Islam Karimov of Uzbekistan. Karimov also attended the following meeting of the Shanghai Five in June of 2001, in Shanghai, at which the Five accepted Uzbekistan as a full member and became — very briefly — the Shanghai Six. On June 15, 2001, the six countries signed the Shanghai Convention on combating terrorism, extremism, and separatism — occasionally referred to as "the three evils" — and finally signed the declaration establishing the SCO and announcing their determination to work on close multilevel cooperation.[13] So from an ad hoc group convened to resolve security consequences from the dissolution of the Soviet Union, the organization evolved into a permanent structure with significant roles over a broad range of economic and security cooperation.

FOLLOWING CHINA AND RUSSIA

The future of the SCO depends largely on the relationship between China and Russia and on where these two major players wish to take the organization. Some future decisions taken by the SCO may be important for the region, but those taken bilaterally by

Beijing and Moscow will be vital. At the same time, the SCO provides a vehicle for Russia and China to cooperate with each other and to observe each other's activity in their area of shared interest in Central Asia. For Russia in particular, the SCO provides an additional multinational group through which it can seek to counter U.S. and Western activity in the region.

Both countries share concern about the continuing U.S. military presence in Central Asia, and both are determined to build a new international order but not (at present) through a force of arms. On July 1, 2005, in Moscow, Presidents Hu Jintao and Vladimir Putin signed the "Joint Statement of the People's Republic of China and the Russian Federation Regarding the International Order of the 21st Century" [sic].[14] To date, this remains the most important joint step taken by the two countries since the signing of the "Treaty of Good-Neighbourliness and Friendly Cooperation between the People's Republic of China and the Russian Federation," on July 16, 2001, a month after the signing of the SCO founding agreement.

The Joint Statement signed by Moscow and Beijing can be taken as a road map for principles of foreign policy for the entire SCO. The first point of the statement warns that "the process of building a new international order will be complicated and lengthy."[15] It continues by declaring that both countries strive to safeguard peace, stability, and security for all of mankind and it vaguely addresses all challenges facing the world, including international terrorism, the proliferation of weapons of mass destruction, organized transnational crime, infectious diseases, and drug trafficking. The statement stresses the importance of the right of the individual countries to choose their own destiny, and noninterference in each other's internal affairs "without resorting to the threat of force or the use of force." The signatories support the United Nations (UN) in a leading role as the creator and executor of the basic norms of international law, and call for strict observation of resolutions of the UN Security Council. They suggest that the UN should be reformed, and should have its "potential for dealing with new challenges and threats enhanced" (Point 3). The statement speaks about human rights "enshrined in the Universal Declaration of Human Rights" but expects individual countries to safeguard them "in [the] light of their own conditions and traditions." It stresses that countries should not interfere in each other's internal affairs and "that the history and traditions of multi-ethnic countries must be respected. Any action aimed at dividing sovereign countries and inciting hatred among ethnic groups is unacceptable" (Points 6 and 7). Russia and China see their new relationship as "a major contribution to building a new international order" and promise to build a new and harmonious world, calling on all countries to engage in extensive dialogue on the issue of the international order of the 21st century (Point 12).[16]

This statement by the two SCO's "senior" members was followed 5 days later by the Declaration of Heads of Member States of SCO, calling on the anti-terrorist coalition in Afghanistan to set a final timeline for their temporary use of the bases and other facilities in the SCO countries.[17] The SCO thereby represents a means through which Russia and China are overcoming their differences in order to work pragmatically toward common interests in a region of shared concern.

As far as the four poorer, landlocked members of the SCO are concerned, this quest by Beijing and Moscow to limit outside influence can be beneficial, as it

7

would tend to preclude external interference in the management of their autocracies (except, of course, by Beijing and Moscow) and promote the kind of stability favored by the local regimes. In pursuing their foreign trade and economic development aims, however, Russia and China cannot always count on the support of other members of the SCO in the same way, since the smaller member states see bilateral economic relations with the United States and other countries outside the organization as beneficial for them and a good bargaining chip in interaction with Beijing and Moscow. Basing agreements with the United States are a specific example of how the interests of the smaller SCO members, and the interests of the United States, may be in direct opposition to the stated priorities of the SCO overall.

SCOPE FOR ENLARGEMENT

A key element of the strategic impact of the emerging SCO, and its implications for U.S. interests, must be the organization's willingness to expand by accepting new applicants for membership—and who those applicants might be. The SCO was not initially prepared to accept any new members. In January 2004, then Russian Minister of Foreign Affairs Igor Ivanov said that the SCO "has to stand on its own feet before it is ready to accept new members."[18] His statement was supported by Chinese Assistant Foreign Minister Li Hui who repeated in June 2004 that the SCO was not ready to accept new members.[19] In October 2005, Zhang Deguang, the SCO's first Executive Secretary— the title of his position was later changed to Secretary General—said that the reason for this was legal since "the appropriate laws were not ready yet."[20] But by May 2006, Zhang Deguang said that the SCO was not a closed organization,[21] and the following month, at the SCO summit, he added that enlargement was possible—but with the continuing rider that appropriate legal work would have to be finalized.[22]

Seven years later, the legal foundation for enlarging the SCO is still not ready. A meeting of Ministries of Foreign Affairs of member states organized by the SCO secretariat in Beijing on April 11-12, 2013, discussed expansion again, as well as work with the observer states and dialogue partners. Once again, the participants "discussed the legal aspects of these issues."[23]

"Observer states" and "dialogue partners" form two distinct groups of states external to the SCO but maintaining relations with it. Both of these statuses were created by Article 14 of the SCO Charter of June 7, 2002, which allows the organization to "interact and maintain dialogue, in certain [unspecified] areas of cooperation, with other states and international organizations" and to "grant a state or international organization concerned the status of a dialogue partner or observer."[24] Belarus and Sri Lanka were granted dialogue partner status at the SCO Summit in 2009, in Yekaterinburg, Russia.[25] Turkey became a dialogue partner at the SCO's 2012 summit in Beijing and apparently wants to upgrade its status to an observer.[26]

Observer status is in theory the shortest (although not necessarily short) route to full membership. Mongolia applied for and received SCO observer status at the SCO Tashkent Summit in 2004.[27] India, Pakistan, and Iran obtained SCO observer status at the Astana Summit in July 2005.[28] The latest observer applicant was Afghanistan, accepted in June 2012 at the Summit in Beijing.[29] According to Chinese and Russian sources, a U.S. application for similar status was rejected in 2005.[30]

Extending membership is likely to continue to prove complex, and prospective members face a range of hurdles. Iranian full membership of the SCO is officially out of the question at the present time because of UN and European Union (EU) sanctions, but also because of Iran's violent international image and its sponsorship of terrorism in many countries. China may be happy to import large quantities of oil from Iran, but accepting Tehran as a full SCO member would seriously dent the organization's international image. While China traditionally has been relatively unrestrained in regard to actions which risk reputational damage for itself, it is more sensitive to the public image of an organization which it is championing as a bastion of regional stability and international cooperation. To introduce a member known to support at least two of the dreaded "three evils" would be problematic.

Iran's self-inflicted precarious situation, in turn, does not help Pakistan toward SCO membership. Pakistan could become an energy and trade corridor to China if the government in Islamabad was able to stabilize the country and to control some of its radical tribes and politicians. Yet, even if Pakistan achieved these seemingly impossible goals, the support of China, its traditional ally, would not be enough: Russia would not accept Islamabad's SCO membership without its own ally, India, being accepted at the same time. India, on the other hand, has major territorial disputes with Pakistan and unresolved border problems with China. In April 2013, the Chinese army had moved into the Depsang Valley in the Ladakh region of eastern Kashmir, 10-km into Indian territory. China claims around 90,000-square-km of land in India's northeastern state of Arunachal Pradesh, while India says China is already occupying 38,000-square-km of territory in the Aksai Chin plateau in the western Himalayas.[31] The two sides have so far held 15 rounds of talks since 1990 to resolve their border dispute,[32] without making much progress, even though China has settled 11 land-based territorial disputes with six other neighbors since 1998.[33]

Belarus's membership of SCO is also unlikely; partly because of Moscow's recurrent confrontations with the mercurial Belarusian President Alyaksandr Lukashenka, and partly because Belarus is clearly a European country whose links with Central Asia and the Far East, despite strenuous efforts by Belarus to pursue a multivector foreign policy, remain extremely modest. Turkey's full membership of the SCO has been discussed mainly because the Turkish Prime Minister Recep Erdogan introduced the subject as an attention-seeking maneuver linked to Turkey's fading campaign to join the EU. Russia is a key energy supplier to Turkey, and there are good trade relations between the two countries. But in June 2009, with Erdogan comparing the plight of the Uighurs—a Turkic-speaking Muslim minority in Xinjiang—to "a kind of genocide," and Turkey's rejection of a dialogue with the Syrian regime—Moscow's close ally—Ankara's SCO candidature looks like a remote prospect.[34] Furthermore, Turkey's SCO membership would also be likely to end its already weak chance of joining the EU, and could potentially complicate its position in NATO.[35]

One of the major problems facing any SCO enlargement process is the incorporation of the new members into the organization's anti-terrorist cooperation structure, and especially its intelligence sharing: every candidate member other than Mongolia brings its own

challenges in terms of trust with one or more existing member states. Intelligence integration and access
in particular would not only be a technical challenge
but also a political one, especially with Iran, Pakistan,
and Afghanistan being granted access to shared intelligence on terrorist organizations.

Of the four countries willing to join the SCO, Mongolia would be the least controversial new member.
However, Mongolia is not confronted by the SCO's
"three evils" (terrorism, extremism, and separatism),
does not need the SCO's help, and has good relations
with both Russia and China, as well as with many
other regional countries. Its present status in the organization may give it sufficient benefits without any
adverse impact on its independence and sovereignty.

For the moment, therefore, any enlargement of
the SCO seems unlikely, since there are obstacles to
the membership of any of the current candidates, and
some (for example, Iran) would instead have a destabilizing effect on the alliance. This, however, does not
prevent the SCO seeking closer links with both observers and partners. After the April 2013 Ministry of
Foreign Affairs (MFA) meeting in Beijing, the SCO has
stated an intention to focus on closer cooperation with
the UN and other international organizations and
with what it describes as "authoritative institutions."[36]

NO THREAT?

Some commentators and analysts see the SCO
as a potential threat and an anti-U.S. coalition.[37] The
latter is to some extent true — the voices from Beijing
and Moscow criticizing the post-Cold War unipolar
world are loud and persistent. The United States and
its democratic allies should expect continuing robust

opposition to some of their policies and initiatives in the UN and other international organizations, especially as Russian foreign policy continues to refine its assertiveness. In addition, the intent toward intensified work with international organizations noted previously may be an indication that the SCO, in a similar manner to the Collective Security Treaty Organization (CSTO), can be used to claim parity or equivalence with U.S.-friendly organizations such as NATO, in an attempt to gain leverage for Russia.

As described later, the uncertain future of Afghanistan will spur SCO member states to even closer cooperation in the field of hard security. In other areas, for example in economic and technical fields, cooperation may be more difficult, in particular because the two "senior members," China and Russia, have widely varying agendas and their world view has little in common except for dislike of U.S. domination. Distrust between these two senior partners is centuries old, and the brief period of communist friendship of the USSR and China between 1949 and the early-1960s cooled quickly and almost immediately turned into hostility during the Cultural Revolution. Even then, the intensity of the friendship was artificially exaggerated by the propaganda machinery of both countries and many Western commentators.

Today, as before, cooperation between the two countries is not as close as official statements from both sides would have us believe. For the time being, China does not appear concerned by what Russia perceives as its slow return toward the center of the international stage, but some officials and experts in Moscow see China's multidirectional growth and Russia's own weaknesses in the Far East as a serious concern. According to Dmitry Rogozin, Russian

Deputy Prime Minister and former Russian ambassador to NATO, between 1993 and 2005 the number of inhabitants in the Russian Far East decreased by 3.7 million and during the same period, the population of Russia decreased by 11 million. He predicts that this trend will continue until 2050 when the population of Russia will drop, in his estimation, to 92-112 million people.[38]

Even without Dr. Rogozin's drastic statistical projections, the situation in the Russian Far East is striking. There are fewer than 7 million inhabitants living in Russia's Far East Federal District,[39] while the other side of the border is inhabited by 100 million Chinese;[40] the population of the three Chinese provinces adjacent to the Russian Far East is more than 20 times the population of the Russian Far East itself, and the entire Russian population east of the Urals is only one and a half times as many as that of "Greater Beijing."[41] Moscow is particularly worried by a potential flood of Chinese immigrants, and its own powerlessness to address the issue. The more alarmist of Russian commentators have long pointed out that, after a general mobilization, the Chinese armed forces would equal Russia's total population.[42] Although it remains unstated in Russian doctrinal documents such as the *National Security Strategy* and *Military Doctrine*, which instead focus on politically acceptable commentary on the supposed threat from NATO,[43] Russia treats the rapid growth of the Chinese armed forces as a potential challenge rather than an immediate threat—while also being annoyed and grudgingly impressed by how quickly the Chinese copied many of the Soviet/Russian weapons exported to China after the collapse of the Soviet Union. Moscow is not worried by an unlikely Chinese military invasion, as it regards its own nuclear force as a sufficient deterrent.[44] However, in spite of the positive noises emanating from both capitals, the two countries still do not trust each other.[45] Rather than building a militarily strong SCO, Russia is interested in strengthening military aspects of the CSTO, set up on October 7, 2002, which also includes four members of the SCO (Russia, Kazakhstan, Kyrgyzstan, and Tajikistan).[46]

The fundamental lack of trust between Moscow and Beijing is not the only internal confidence problem within the SCO, which suffers from a complex web of mutual mistrust between member states. There are still serious border disagreements and ethnic tensions between Uzbekistan and Kyrgyzstan. Relations between Uzbekistan and Tajikistan are also not friendly, and strained by the proposed completion of a controversial dam built in a seismically dangerous area and exacerbating issues of water politics. Periodic gas cut-offs from Uzbekistan render Tajikistan vulnerable and are also not conducive to improvement in bilateral relations. In 2012, Uzbekistan introduced exit visas for Uzbek passport holders who want to visit Tajikistan, in an attempt to limit links between the two countries.[47]

Furthermore, there are increasingly visible frictions between Moscow and Dushanbe. Tajikistan, the poorest of the Central Asian countries, is trying to capitalize on the changing situation in Afghanistan by improving its relations with the United States,[48] and Moscow is unhappy with Dushanbe's diplomatic efforts to improve its relations with Washington. Igor Shuvalov, Russia's First Deputy Prime Minister, and Colonel General Valery Gerasimov, Chief of the Russian General Staff, both recently postponed visits to Dushanbe.[49] Both countries agreed that Russia would modernize the Tajik armed forces without Russia paying for their "201st Base" (the former 201st Motor-Rifle Division, stationed on the Tajik-Afghan border) in Tajikistan. Dushanbe requested more than the offered $200 million plus an additional $200 million worth of fuel, perhaps encouraged by the knowledge that neighboring Kyrgyzstan is expecting $1.1 billion from Moscow for the modernization of its forces.[50] Anecdotal evidence suggests that Central Asian states are more impressed with the quality, efficiency, and efficacy of U.S. military training and equipment assistance than its Russian equivalent; but Russian offers come without the troublesome overhead of external interest in domestic human rights issues, and consequences such as the withholding of aid following mass deaths of civilians during unrest in Andijan, Uzbekistan, in May 2005.[51]

Tajikistan is therefore trying to improve its relations with Washington, in part in the hope of keeping some of the military hardware left behind by the drawdown from Afghanistan. This may be a very risky strategy because Russia is in a position to destabilize Tajikistan by influencing, or even removing, the large number of Tajik migrant laborers working in Russia who provide remittances that shore up the Tajik economy.[52] The implications for U.S. bilateral relations, and for potential basing arrangements in particular, are clear: the willingness by Tajikistan's leadership to engage in balancing between the major powers continues to present the United States with opportunities to exploit, as it has done since the early days of the current intervention in Afghanistan.[53] At the same time, the example of Ayni airbase in Tajikistan, still unused almost a decade after India began its redevelopment and announced plans for basing there, shows how successful intervention can be mounted to prevent a foreign military presence in the country.[54]

In the coming years, Russia and China plan to continue substantially strengthening their armed forces, and both countries are likely to continue to make statements separately, jointly, or with the SCO which directly and indirectly criticize aspects of U.S. and NATO policies. The SCO Summit in June 2012 in Beijing gives an example of the tone. The heads of member states declared that the:

> unilateral and unlimited build-up of anti-missile defence, by one state or group of states, without taking into account the legitimate interests of other countries may damage international security and strategic stability in the world,

and called to resolve this destabilizing process by political and diplomatic effort.[55] The subject is clearly of immediate concern to Moscow, some interest to Beijing, and no relevance whatsoever to the other SCO members. Despite the strong wording of the statement, it will have no impact on the organization's defense planning or military capability.

Occasional speculation in its early days that the SCO could become a military bloc was addressed in June 2005 by Russian Foreign Minister Sergey Lavrov. He rejected the idea, adding that the organization does not even plan to form a rapid deployment force.[56] One year later, Executive Secretary Zhang Deguang denied that the organization was the eastern equivalent of NATO, adding that "the SCO will never become a military bloc."[57] Nothing since has indicated that the SCO's plans or attitude have changed in this respect. Russia and China will build up their armed forces for years to come, but they will do so separately.

FUTURE PLANS AND CONTEMPORARY REALITIES

In common with other international bodies, the SCO can on occasion produce a great deal more rhetoric than action. At a meeting of SCO heads of states on October 14, 2009, in Beijing, member states agreed on 15 principal points, including:

- The need to ensure the economic stability of the member states and improving their economic cooperation, to overcome the global financial and economic crisis.
- The necessity to strengthen the financial cooperation within the organization.
- Improving the role of the SCO Business Council and to focus on the preparation of proposals for the implementation of joint regional projects.
- Instructing the appropriate ministries and agencies to take the necessary measures for more effective use of existing transit potential of the SCO member states, further improvement of the transport infrastructure, and strengthening the legal framework for transport cooperation.
- Calling for early launch of pilot projects such as the "SCO information superhighway" (of which no details have yet been publicly released) and to establish secure electronic cross-border links.
- The need to stress the importance of agricultural cooperation.
- Reaffirming the importance of scientific and technical cooperation within the SCO, especially in the priority areas of scientific and technological innovations.

- The active promotion of practical cooperation between the SCO member states and observer states of the SCO.
- The determination to improve the medical and cultural cooperation between the member states.[58]

And yet, the participants did not offer any specific policies or propose any actual undertakings.

In addition to meetings of political, administrative, foreign policymaking, security organs, and law enforcement bodies, the SCO Secretariat organizes and coordinates meetings of an impressive array of interstate groups, covering a range of activities, some of which are far removed from the organization's original focus on hard security issues. These include meetings of unspecified "financial organs" (most recently April 23-24, 2012, in Shanghai), the SCO Economic Forums/Fora (April 23-24, 2012, in Almaty and April 18, 2013, in Beijing), meetings of the Chairmen of the National Supreme Courts (April 23-25, 2012, in Beijing), meetings of the SCO Ministers of Defence (April 24, 2012, in Beijing), Ministers of Finances and Heads of the National Banks (May 16-17, 2012, in Beijing), Ministers of Culture (June 4-7, 2012), Attorneys-General (June 5-6, 2012, in Dushanbe), and the "5th SCO Discussion Club," which included participants from the United Kingdom (UK) and Germany (March 14, 2013, in Beijing).

Many of these meetings are no more than diplomatic familiarization tours and public relations exercises with little actual substance, and it remains unclear whether any of them, in fact, have the bureaucratic capacity to achieve any actual deliverables. The

9th meeting of the SCO Culture Ministers, in Beijing in early June 2012, provides a good example. Participants praised the mechanism of these annual meetings, and expressed their satisfaction with its friendly and constructive spirit, mutual understanding, and trust. They "exchanged opinions on the implementation of the Plan of Activities for 2009-2011" and discussed "further strengthening cultural cooperation in the SCO framework in the coming decade." They agreed to "deepen cooperation in the field of protection of historic cultural heritage" and to "stimulate cooperation in the field of culture and maintain cultural exchanges with the SCO observer and dialogue partner countries."[59] Yet, in common with many other SCO meetings on topics other than security and law enforcement, the SCO Culture Ministers have been engaging in these meetings since 2002 with no visible achievement as a result.

RATS

A Complicated Birth . . .

By contrast, antiterrorism cooperation by SCO states shows distinct signs of productive activity. The first meeting of the Shanghai Five security and law enforcement officials in Bishkek in December 1999 was Moscow's first serious attempt to set up an anti-terrorist substructure for the organization, the "Regional Anti-Terrorist Structure" (RATS). Three years later, at the SCO foreign ministers' extraordinary meeting in Beijing on January 7, 2002, the candidature of Bishkek as a location for this structure was accepted,[60] and Article 10 of the Shanghai Charter, signed in St. Petersburg on June 7, 2002, confirmed that "the Regional Counter-Terrorist Structure established by the member States of the Shanghai Convention" would be located in Bishkek in the Kyrgyz Republic.[61]

This, however, did not come about, causing considerable private embarrassment within the SCO at the time.[62] Strong support for Russia's initiative from Kyrgyz President Askar Akayev was not enough to bring the project to life. China and Uzbekistan, opponents of the project, argued that the world had changed after the September 11, 2001, attacks, Kyrgyzstan was in turmoil, and there was concern that a Kyrgyzstan-based RATS HQ would be dominated by Russia. China and Uzbekistan were also ambivalent about Moscow's efforts to strengthen the CSTO, as evidenced by the fact that Uzbekistan left the organization in April 1999, and China never joined it; in fact, in the form of the CSTO, Russia was attempting to build up a parallel anti-terrorist structure and militarize it, while the negotiations to set up the RATS went on. Tashkent was especially discontented with Moscow's attempts to dominate the RATS, and because Russia was seen as siding with Bishkek in the ongoing conflict between Kyrgyz and Uzbek ethnic groups. The internal conflict in Kyrgyzstan was a powerful argument to move the RATS HQ to another country, and the SCO's Prime Ministers, with the approval of their Heads of States, signed off on a new anti-terrorist center in Tashkent on September 23, 2003.[63] The RATS began to operate on January 1, 2004, and the official launch of its Executive Committee took place on June 17, 2004, also in Tashkent,[64] under its first Executive Director, Major General Vyacheslav Temirovich Kasymov, Deputy Chairman of the Uzbek National Security Service.[65]

The birth complications of the RATS continued, deepening the apprehension of some of SCO members as Major General Suhrob Kasymov used a conference in Beijing in the summer of 2004 to criticize the CSTO.[66] In February 2005, Suhrob Kasymov publicly criticized Kazakhstan's insufficient determination to combat terrorism on its own soil[67] — an accusation naturally rejected by the Kazakh MFA. Yet, this was the last time when a disagreement among members of the RATS came into public view. The artificial cordiality that has been observed since may not have been difficult to maintain in public: the SCO is a nontransparent organization, of which Russia, with its muscular democracy, is by far the most democratic — or least undemocratic — member, so concealing any disagreements or shortcomings from public view should not prove difficult.

The original stated function of the RATS was to maintain working contacts and coordinate the activities of the relevant organs of the SCO member states in combating terrorism, extremism, and separatism. At the outset, the RATS employed 30 people — seven from Russia, seven from China, six from Kazakhstan, five from Uzbekistan, three from Kyrgyzstan, and three from Tajikistan. The original budget of the organization was about $2 million, of which 24 percent each came from China and Russia, 21 percent paid by Kazakhstan, 15 percent by Uzbekistan, 10 percent by Kyrgyzstan, and 6 percent by Tajikistan.[68] Information about its present budget and the number of employees is classified.

... and a bright future?

The RATS claims a consistent record of success in combating terrorism, but it is not always clear how much of this is thanks to the RATS itself rather than to the individual and uncoordinated efforts of its member countries. For instance, according to Vyacheslav Kasymov, in 2005 the special services of the SCOs countries "prevented 263 terrorist acts, killing or arresting 15 leaders of extremist organizations" including extremist groups planning suicide attacks against the U.S. embassy and other targets — claimed as a success for the RATS less than a year after its formation.[69]

By early-2006 the RATS investigative register contained about 800 names of members of terrorist groups, which were to be added to its new database.[70] Five years later, in 2011, the RATS reportedly contributed to more than 400 arrests of terrorist suspects in the SCO countries, and prevented 10 terrorist acts and about 200 other unspecified actions. More than 400 terrorists were killed; more than 480 individuals belonging to forbidden organizations were detained; and six terrorist groups, eight religious extremists groups, and two unspecified gangs "were eliminated."[71]

Despite building operational capabilities and conducting several anti-terrorist exercises since the early days of its existence, the RATS has never attempted to build its own anti-terrorist force or coordinate the armed forces of member states in formations or units capable of operating against terrorist groups. Turning RATS into a joint military organization, or establishing an entirely new SCO military structure, would require political will, large-scale defense investment, and a level of coordination which Beijing and Moscow would have difficulty in sustaining, due to political rather than technical reasons.

At present, the RATS is still developing what may potentially be its most powerful tool, an international terrorism intelligence sharing database. As well as collection from online, electronic, and print media, the database receives information from the RATS member states and other SCO agencies. In return, the RATS Executive Committee transmits a quarterly report on information acquired by the database to the security and law enforcement organizations of the member states. The agreement on the database stipulates that only authorized officials of the RATS member states will have access to it, with access granted by order of the RATS Executive Committee. Significantly, the working languages of the database project are Russian and Chinese:[72] a Russian company was responsible for initial database development and information security, and additional software was developed by a Chinese firm.[73]

The database's content supposedly includes information about terrorist, separatist, and extremist organizations, their structures, their operational methods, their leaders and other individuals involved in these organizations, as well as sources and channels of funding, including the trafficking of illicit drugs and their ingredients. It also stores information about organizations and individuals which support terrorism, extremism, and separatism, potential measures to counter them, and information on legislation affecting individual member states and international organizations. Analysis of terrorist acts includes information on the equipment and materials used, including explosives and components.

Gradual improvement of anti-terrorist cooperation within the RATS can be considered a success, not only because (considering the lack of trust among certain member states) the decision to share some elements of anti-terrorist information must have been preceded by lengthy, complex, and secret talks, but also because it represents an entirely new technological and security network which the member states had to cooperate to set up. The extent of technological and security co-ordination required in managing the RATS database, and indeed in granting and controlling access, may have presented a steep learning curve for some of the smaller member states.

Relative to other SCO activities, internal coopera-tion within the RATS appears unusually productive, and since cooperation is clearly in the best interests of the ruling regimes of the contributing states, it is very probable that the member states will continue working on its improvement. Furthermore, the RATS is highly likely to be a beneficiary of the intense con-cern shared by SCO member states over the aftermath of the International Security Assistance Force (ISAF) drawdown in Afghanistan.

SCO countries are critical of the ISAF presence in Afghanistan, saying that it achieves more harm than good, and yet simultaneously is deeply apprehensive of the consequences of the ISAF drawdown for the region after 2014. Russia claims that heroin produc-tion in Afghanistan has increased 40 times since 2001, and quotes UN statistics from 2012 indicating that Afghanistan produces about 90 percent of the world's opium. Russia also maintains that about 15 percent of Afghanistan's gross national product depends on drug-related exports, which amounts to a business worth U.S.$2.4 billion a year. Qayum Samir, spokes-man for Afghanistan's Counternarcotics Ministry, an-nounced at the beginning of April 2013 that 157,000 hectares of poppies are being planted in Afghanistan this year—3,000 hectares more than in 2012.[74]

All the SCO states expect to be targeted by new and resurrected terrorist groups, and subjected to an increased flow of narcotics, post-2014. Each of them can therefore be expected to invest in their counter-terrorist organizations, special services, organizations combating drug trafficking, and border guards, and to develop international cooperation, including through the means of the RATS. A meeting of the organizations responsible for combating drug trafficking and other "competent organs" of the SCO took place in Bishkek on April 30, 2013. As expected, the participants of the meeting discussed the problems of combating the illicit trafficking of drugs and their precursors, focusing on how to counter the production and trafficking of opium from Afghanistan. The meeting approved an Action Plan for 2013-14 in accordance with the Anti-Drug Strategy of the SCO member states for the years 2011-16.[75] No details of the Plan or the Strategy were made public.

Key Facts.

The RATS is directed by two principal bodies: the Executive Committee and the Council. The RATS Executive Committee deals with three principal tasks:

1. Information and analytical support of security and law enforcement bodies of the member states, consisting mainly of the creation and maintenance of a joint database on international terrorist organizations and their members. In 2009, the SCO considered setting up a special information file within the RATS's anti-terrorist database which would hold information about illegal arms, ammunition, and explosives.[76]

2. Coordinating the fight against terrorism, extremism, and separatism.

3. International legal work relevant to the RATS's activities.

The Council meets twice a year to provide strategic directions and plans for the Committee. The Council is the transmission belt between national decisionmakers, national security organizations, and the RATS Executive Committee. Its Chairmen are usually hidden from the public eye, as they are serving as high ranking security officials in their own countries. During its March 29, 2013, meeting in Tashkent, the Council approved a draft protocol between the SCO RATS and the Commonwealth of Independent States (CIS) Anti-Terrorism Centre, on the organization of cooperation on the security of major international events held on the territories of the SCO and the CIS. The participants agreed also to hold an international conference on strengthening cooperation in the field of information security.[77]

The RATS main functions are:

- To maintain working contacts with the relevant organs of member states and international organizations dealing with terrorism, extremism, and separatism.
- To promote interaction among member states in organizing and conducting exercises at the request of the member states concerned, preparations and conduct of operational-search and other activities to fight terrorism, extremism, and separatism.
- Participating in the drafting of international legal documents affecting the fight against terrorism, extremism, and separatism.
- Collection and analysis of information received by the RATS from member states and forming and updating the RATS's database.
- Participation in the formation of an effective system to address global challenges and threats.

- Preparing and conducting scientific conferences and seminars, and promoting the exchange of experience in the fight against terrorism, extremism, and separatism.[78]

OUTLOOK

Both China and Russia may have misgivings about U.S. policies and U.S. military presence in Asia, but it would take extraordinary and unexpected events to convince them of the need to militarize the SCO. Both countries work consistently on strengthening SCO anti-terrorist cooperation, and they will continue to do so because of the uncertain future of Afghanistan and the possible rebirth of radical Islamic groups across the whole region. At the SCO Bishkek meeting of Security Councils of the member states of the SCO at the end of April 2013, Chinese representative State Councilor Guo Shengkun announced that the new Chinese leadership will fully support law enforcement and security body cooperation within the SCO.[79] This statement from the SCO's principal and most dynamic stakeholder does not necessarily mean that cooperation in other areas will improve correspondingly.

Ambitious statements by the SCO are rarely followed up with specific plans. This may be because the organization itself has very limited capacity. The SCO is reluctant to discuss the financial aspects of its plans or even its budget, but if older figures quoted by some, usually Russian, commentators are to be believed, the budget of the organization is very small. According to one source, in 2006 the SCO budget was $3.5 million, increasing to $3.7 million in 2007, with funding contributions divided between member states in the same proportions as for funding the RATS as described previously—Russia and China providing 24 percent each; Kazakhstan, 21 percent; Uzbekistan, 15 percent; Kyrgyzstan, 10 percent; and Tajikistan, 6 percent. The same source said that the SCO's budget for 2008, approved by the heads of the member states on November 2, 2007, was to be $3.5 million.[80] Other sources give figures which are similarly small for such a large organization.[81] These modest sums are in stark contrast to the projected budget for the preparation of the SCO summit in Ufa, Russia, in 2015, set by the local authorities at 60 billion rubles (approximately $1.8 billion).[82]

Any closer economic cooperation within the SCO is likely to encounter serious difficulty. Although all the leaders of the SCO member states are in a position to influence just about every economic decision taken at the national level in their countries—without paying attention to their parliaments, the judiciary, the media, or their internal opponents—even they would have problems if they were to return to the old communist model of large-scale money-losing "investments" in the SCO's poorer members, without dramatic and visible political or social benefits. Kazakhstan, Uzbekistan, Kyrgyzstan, and Tajikistan must also be concerned that closer economic cooperation within the framework of the SCO will attach them too strongly to the two larger members, especially China, and could thereby limit their potential political and economic contacts with the United States, the EU, Japan, and other countries. At the same time, this does not rule out continued significant investment in Central Asian states by China, as keen to acquire influence there through economic means as Russia is to retain it through military cooperation and basing.

Long-term mutual economic investment by SCO states in Central Asia may also encounter political problems. Kyrgyzstan, the most democratic and the least stable of the four countries, has already experienced two coups this century, in March 2005 and April 2010. In 2012, Kyrgyzstan ranked 154th on the Transparency International corruption list among 176 listed countries.[83] The three remaining Central Asian states are run by fiercely independent dictators, not ready to relinquish their power or prepare their countries for less dictatorial systems. Uzbekistan, Kazakhstan, and Tajikistan have no visible generation of new leaders being groomed to replace their current leaders. The gradual, eventual departure of these three leaders from politics, or from this world, may result in dangerous local political vacuums and internal conflicts with the potential to destabilize the whole region. All four countries are geostrategically very important but, at this stage of their development, have little else to offer, including their natural resources and their markets. All four current Central Asian leaders may be attracted by some aspect of the Chinese dynamic economy, but they and their countries' links with Russia are much stronger than with China. Russia, however, with the exception of oil and weapons, also has little to offer in comparison with the United States, the West, the Far East, and, increasingly, Brazil.

At the 8th SCO Bishkek forum on April 18, 2013, the organization's experts recommended stronger cooperation programs in areas such as medical care, modernization of the railway system, and public service. Experts taking part in the forum suggested also that some aspects of the SCO cooperation should be devolved from the governmental level to nongovernmental organizations (NGOs). This change could considerably complicate economic cooperation inside the SCO, because all SCO member states fight ongoing, but largely unsuccessful, battles against corruption. Yet, the decision to set up a SCO banking system and the SCO Development Fund were of political rather than financial importance,[84] and the Fund itself was originally opposed by Russia.[85] When and how the new banking system and the Fund are to operate is as yet unspecified.

There is a precedent for this kind of activity in the form of Brazil, Russia, India, China, and South Africa (BRICS) financial cooperation, which, of course, also involves both China and Russia; one key difference, however, is the considerable economic power wielded by each of the individual BRICS members in their own right, very dissimilar to the unbalanced nature of the SCO where the economies of the smaller members are almost invisible by comparison with Russia and China. Intimidating sounding statistics about the SCO's land area, total population, or geostrategy do not reflect the organization's imperfect cohesion, or the real capabilities, intentions, and ambitions of the individual member states or their future plans. Economically, the SCO as a whole is of very little significance compared to the individual weight of its two senior members.

Nevertheless, the SCO will remain a major security player in Central Asia in large part simply because its individual members are determined to protect their interests in this volatile region. The organization does not intend, at least for the time being, to build military power because there is no perceived need for it; the smaller members would depend entirely on Russia and/or China, and these two larger members are capable of addressing their immediate defense challenges without outside help and do not trust each other sufficiently to build a functional military bloc.

The departure of ISAF forces from Afghanistan will not change the SCO's attitude towards the United States and its allies—all the more so if the United States or its allies retain any military facilities on Afghan soil. Moscow is deeply concerned about any continuing U.S. military presence in greater Central Asia. Nikolay Patrushev, Russian Security Council Secretary, said that Russia opposes any foreign presence in Afghanistan which may be used against other countries.[86] Withdrawal of equipment from Afghanistan post-2014 through SCO member countries will remain a fragile option. A less critical attitude toward the political imperfections of the Central Asian leaders and their lack of democratic credentials, supported by large-scale financial and long-term political initiatives, would not only continue to safeguard this process, but could potentially reduce the psychological dependence of the four smaller members of the SCO on China and Russia.

The United States, NATO, Japan, South Korea, and India should have long-term and well planned security, economic, and cultural cooperation policies in place for individual countries of Central Asia. At the same time, criticism of any level of engagement in the region should be expected from the media and from single-issue NGOs. The scope of direct cooperation on counterterrorism may be limited by the very different local definitions of terrorism, and approaches to counterterror operations and collateral damage, from the U.S. and Western norms. In an interview in 2006, RATS Executive Director Kasymov noted that during meetings with Western partners, SCO members "hear a lot about threats and challenges, but as soon as it comes to practical measures against terrorists, they begin to talk about 'excessive force'."[87]

Moscow and Beijing will continue to work jointly to limit U.S. influence in the UN and international organizations. They may be supported in international fora by individual members of the SCO, paying their "club membership" political fee, but no joint actions, diplomatic or other, should be expected from the organization. At the same time, Russia may support China but would not get involved in any of Beijing's conflicts, and vice versa. SCO smaller member states, with enough of their own economic and security challenges to address, can be expected to attempt to avoid involvement in faraway international disputes.

In addition, Moscow and possibly Beijing may seek to leverage SCO support in order to claim parity or equivalence with U.S.-friendly organizations such as NATO, in a similar pattern to that currently seen with the CSTO.

Implications and Policy Recommendations.

China's immediate approaches to Central Asian states directly after the fall of the Soviet Union testify to Beijing's long-standing commitment to expanding economic and natural resource harvesting opportunities in the region. At the same time, Moscow traditionally views Central Asia as its own sphere of interest, and has a strong desire to maintain political influence including keeping the U.S. out of the region. As the United States continues to develop interests and policies for the region, these two opposing forces will be the main challenge. However, mutual mistrust not only between Russia and China but also between the smaller SCO members presents the U.S. with opportunities to exploit the Central Asian states' differences in policy and interest from Moscow and Beijing.

Current U.S. policy objectives in Central Asia include stability for Afghanistan, combating terrorism, stemming drug flow, and non-proliferation. These policy goals are closely aligned with the stated SCO goals, which bring an opportunity to pursue these policies on a bilateral basis with each country without public resistance. Most Central Asian states value their bilateral relationships with the U.S. simply because of the financial incentives it provides. However, any financial assistance with strings attached to human rights, democratization, or combating corruption will be met with resistance, and will likely hinder the development of close political ties and alliances within Central Asia. It should be remembered that attempts to link aid, assistance or cooperation with domestic governance issues, and in particular human rights, will immediately increase the relative attractiveness of Russian and Chinese offerings.

There are direct implications for the future of basing arrangements and broader bilateral security cooperation with the Central Asian states. According to the U.S. Department of State, it was bilateral exchanges with the five Central Asian states that resulted in the establishment of the Northern Distribution Network (NDN), the network of roads, railroads, rivers, and ports in use by the U.S. military to move equipment from Afghanistan. The U.S. Army alone is scheduled to move 80,000 containers and 20,000 vehicles out of Afghanistan by December 2014, much of which will rely on the NDN. The political will of these countries to continue to support the NDN through 2014 is strong, but any U.S. extended presence beyond 2014 is likely to encounter stronger resistance, as Moscow steps in to ensure the U.S. departs the area on time.

Risks to U.S. interests in Central Asia arise from Russian influence as opposed to SCO policies. Russia has a vested interest in removing a U.S. presence from Central Asia, and will use all tools at its disposal toward this aim, including the SCO. This is in addition to bilateral leverage, which Russia possesses to different extents against different states. This is demonstrated by the example of Uzbekistan, which enjoys close relations with the United States and blows hot and cold on security cooperation with Russia and Russia-dominated supranational entities like the SCO, CSTO and Eurasian Union. Bilaterally, the benefits of security cooperation with Russia can be immediate and tangible for Central Asian regimes, as with the example of Russian support for President Rahmonov of Tajikistan in his election campaign in exchange for continued Tajik facilitation of the Russian "201st Base" there.

Consequently, decisionmakers considering future options for basing arrangements in Central Asia should observe closely the instance of Manas, a U.S. military logistics hub located near the Kyrgyz capital, Bishkek. The history of confrontation over Manas provides a valuable case study of the range of public, private, and clandestine influences which can be brought to bear on host nations by Russia. In addition to direct financial competition, over a number of years Moscow increased pressure on the Kyrgyz government to close the base, including several security and economic bilateral accords designed to project exclusive Russian influence in Kyrgyzstan. Most recently, at the time of this writing, the Kyrgyz parliament voted to terminate the lease just a few days after Russian President Vladimir Putin visited Bishkek.

If the U.S. Army wishes to maintain a presence in Central Asia post-2014, strong opposition from Russia can be expected unless a deal is brokered whereby that presence can be portrayed as meeting Russian interests. For example, Russia wishes to arrive at a situation where the United States is explicitly bound by international agreements, since this is one of the few areas where Russia can exert leverage. This leads to a desire to tie any U.S. presence in Afghanistan, and by extension in its Central Asian supply route, to a UN Security Council resolution—in other words, to have the UN regulate and govern the U.S. presence post-2014. Under these circumstances, Russia would accept the enhanced security and assistance with counterterrorism and counternarcotics programs which a U.S. presence in the Central Asian SCO states could provide.

As noted previously, the prospects for SCO expansion are limited, despite a number of countries expressing interest in joining. Although SCO accession by either Iran or Turkey is not an immediate prospect, both these potential developments should be watched closely. In particular, Turkey's NATO membership brings immediate complications and a potential conflict of interest if security cooperation with the SCO states is increased.

Large-scale joint anti-terrorist exercises by the armed forces of SCO states are likely to become more frequent. Because of the very different definitions of terrorism and counterterror operations noted earlier, some of these may resemble the beginning of SCO military cooperation, especially if there is a resurgence of radical, armed Islamic groups in the region. In particular, a "bloc law enforcement and security apparatus" intended to counter terrorism and narcotics may strongly resemble military cooperation, and will certainly have direct implications for security cooperation with the United States. But this should not be treated by the United States as the creation of a military bloc, unless specific evidence and intentions to the contrary appear.

When considering the SCO, U.S. policymakers should view it primarily as a vehicle to further Russian interests in Central Asian states and beyond. To Russia, the SCO is one tool for the overall purpose of countering U.S. policy. Other, similar tools include the CSTO, CIS, BRICS, and the Eurasian Union.

Russia gains political support from these supranational organizations to rally for Russian interests. Forum shopping and influence peddling is a key tactic for Russia in its current weakened state; the goal is to use political leverage to influence international norms to reflect Russian interests, change the course of how the world thinks, and reflect what Russia wants from the world. Russian, as well as Chinese, initiatives in fora such as the UN can rely on support from other SCO members.

At the same time, specific policy aims of the SCO, or Russia through the SCO, should not be analyzed according to U.S. policy criteria. It is not necessary for an event to take place that would be considered by the United States as a substantial policy achievement, in order for Russia to believe that the SCO has contributed to countering U.S. aims as part of an overall strategy. There may well be no single reason for specific SCO actions: the tradition in the region of planning the "kombinatsiya," or cascade effect with multiple possible objectives, is strong.[88]

This allowance for multiple possible outcomes can make it challenging for U.S. policymakers to discern the longer-term, patient strategy employed by Russia through implements such as the SCO. Instead of thinking in terms of direct linkages, where action X leads to consequence Y, many of the aims of establishing and developing the SCO are less well-defined and consist more of building long-term policy momentum for long-term aims, including eroding the U.S. near-monopoly on moral support and on the ability to marshal backers in international fora. Thus, the apparent lack of concrete achievements by the SCO as an international organization should not lead U.S. policymakers to discount it as a tool, or facilitator, for longer-term objectives by its two key members.

ENDNOTES

1. January 2, Uzbekistan; January 3, Kazakhstan; January 4, Tajikistan; January 5, Kyrgyzstan; and January 6, Turkmenistan. K. S. Anufriyev, *Politika Rossii i Kitaya v Tsentralnoy Aziy* (*Politics of Russia and China in Central Asia*), Tomsk, Russia: Izdatelstvo Tomskogo Universiteta, 2011, p. 121.

2. In February 1992, Kazakh Prime Minister Sergey Tereshchenko visited China. Uzbek President Karimov visited Beijing in March 1992; his Kyrgyz counterpart, Akayev, went to China in May, and Turkmen president Niyazov in November 1992. All the Central Asian visitors signed several agreements with China.

3. Yuriy Mikhaylovich Galenovich, *Istoriya Otnosheniy Rossii i Kitaya* (*History of Relations Between Russia and China*), Moscow, Russia: Russkaya Panorama, 2011, pp. 51-67.

4. Anufriyev, pp. 124-125.

5. The agreement was ratified by China's Standing Committee of the National People's Congress in April 2005 and by the Russian State Duma in May 2005. On June 2, 2005, the Russian and Chinese Foreign Ministers exchanged the ratification documents.

6. "China, Russia Complete Border Survey, Determination," *Xinhua*, July 21, 2008, available from *news.xinhuanet.com/english/2008-07/21/content_8739941.htm;* "China, Russia Solve All Border Disputes," *Xinhua*, June 2, 2005, available from *news.xinhuanet.com/english/2005-06/02/content_3037975.htm.*

7. Anufriyev, p. 125.

8. *Ibid.*, p. 122.

9. Yu. S. Peskov, "Problemy i Perspektyvy Sotrudnichestva Rossii i Kitaya so Stranami Tsentralnoy Azii – Chlenami SNG" ("Problems and Prospects of Cooperation of China and Russia with the Central Asian States which are Members of the CIS"), *Problemy Dalnego Vostoka,* 1997, No. 3, p. 53.

10. Yu.S. Peskov, "Problemy i Perspektyvy Sotrudnichestva Rossii i Kitaya so Stranami Tsentralnoy Azii – Chlenami SNG" ("Problems and Prospects of Cooperation of China and Russia with the Central Asian States which are Members of the CIS"), *Problemy Dalnego Vostoka,* 1997, No. 4, p. 22.

11. Diplomaticheskiy Vestnik (A Multilateral Meeting in Almaty), August 1998, available from *www.mid.ru/ bdomp/dip_vest.nsf/19c2fdee616f12e54325688e00486a45/c603b 3915829207dc32568890029bb34.*

12. Gill Bates and Mathew Oreseman, "China's New Journey to the West: China's Emergence in Central Asia and Implications for US Interests," Washington, DC: Center for Strategic and International Studies (CSIS), 2003, p. 7.

13. For the original goals of the SCO, see: "Brief introduction to the Shanghai Cooperation Organisation," SCO website, available from *www.sectsco.org/EN123/brief.asp.*

14. Asia Adam Wofe, "Cool-headed diplomacy," *Asia Times Online*, August 6, 2005, available from *www.atimes.com/atimes/ Central_Asia/GH06Ag02.html*

15. "China, Russia Call for Multilateralism in World Affairs," *Xinhua*, July 1, 2005, available from *news.xinhuanet.com/ english/2005-07/01/content_3164071.htm.*

16. "China, Russia Issue Joint Statement on New World Order," *Xinhua*, July 1, 2005, available from *news.xinhuanet.com/ english/2005-07/01/content_3164427.htm.*

17. "SCO Leaders Vow to Boost Group's Internal Construction," *People.com*, July 6, 2005, available from *english.people.com. cn/200507/06/eng20050706_194332.html*.

18. "Interview of Secretary of the Russian Security Council Igor Ivanov with the Russian News & Information Agency RIA Novosti," *RIA Novosti*, May 22, 2007, available from *en.ria.ru/ analysis/20070522/65587920.html*.

19. "Chinese Official Says SCO Not Ready To Accept New Member," *Xinhua*, June 1, 2004.

20. "SCO Not To Admit New Members Presently: Executive Secretary," *Xinhua*, October 27, 2005.

21. "SCO Remains Open Organisation—Secretary-General," UzReport Information Agency, June 6, 2006, available from *mir. uzreport.uz/news_e_13423.html*.

22. "Joint Communiqué of Meeting of the Council of the Heads of the Member States of the Shanghai Cooperation Organisation," June 15, 2006, SCO official website for SCO Summit of 2013, available from *www.scosummit2013.org/en/documents/english-joint-communique-of-meeting-of-the-council-of-the-heads-of-the-member-states-of-the-shanghai-cooperation-organisation/*.

23. "*O mezhmidovskikh konsultatsiyakh po voprosam rasshireniya Organizatsii*" ("On Inter-Foreign-Ministries Consultations on the Expansion of the Organisation"), SCO website, April 12, 2013, available from *www.sectsco.org/RU123/show.asp?id=597*.

24. "Charter of the Shanghai Cooperation Organization," SCO official website for SCO Summit of 2013, June 7, 2002, available from *www.scosummit2013.org/en/documents/hartiya-shanhaykoy-organizatsii-sotrudnichestva/*.

25. *China Daily*, June 16, 2009, available from *www.chinadaily. com.cn/china/2009sco/200906/16/content_8289713.htm*.

26. "Turkey Seeks Observer Member Status in SCO," *Hurriyet Daily News*, February 1, 2013, available from *www.hurriyetdaily-*

*news.com/turkey-seeks-observer-member-status-in-sco.aspx?pageID=2
38&nID=40267&NewsCatID=338.*

27. "Tashkent Summit Marks New Phase for SCO," *China Daily*, June 18, 2004, available from *www.chinadaily.com.cn/english/ doc/2004-06/18/content_340361.htm.*

28. "Fifth Summit in Astana 2005," *People's Daily Online*, July 26, 2007, available from *english.people.com. cn/90002/91620/91644/6224952.html.*

29. "Press Communiqué of the Meeting of the Council of The Heads of the Member States of The Shanghai Cooperation Organization," Ministry of Foreign Affairs of the People's Republic of China website, June 6-7, 2012, available from *www.fmprc.gov.cn/ eng/wjdt/2649/t939161.shtml.*

30. Yang Hongxi, "The Evolution of the U.S. Attitude towards the SCO," Beijing, China: China Center For Contemporary World Studies, March 14, 2013, available from *www.cccws.org.cn/en/News-Info.aspx?NId=2311.* See also Ariel Cohen, "What to Do About the Shanghai Cooperation Organization's Rising Influence," *Eurasianet*, September 20, 2006, available from *www.eurasianet.org/ departments/insight/articles/eav092106.shtml;* and Vladimir Fedoruk, "Russia, China don't see US in SCO," *Voice of Russia*, November 1, 2011, available from *voiceofrussia.com/2011/11/01/59706557/.*

31. Arti Bali, "China's New Twist to the Border Issue," *Samay Live*, May 12, 2013, available from *english.samaylive.com/nation-news/articles/676529525/china-s-new-twist-to-the-border-issue.html.*

32. Rama Lakshami, "India-China Border Dispute: Both Sides Step Warily with High-Level Visits Due," *The Guardian*, May 7, 2013, available from *www.guardian.co.uk/world/2013/may/07/india-china-border-dispute.*

33. "India-China Border Tensions Remain: Pentagon," NDTV, May 7, 2013, available from *www.ndtv.com/article/india/india-china-border-tensions-remain-pentagon-363521; The Times of India*, May 6, 2013, available from *articles.timesofindia.indiatimes.com/2013-05-06/ india/39063666_1_defence-capabilities-daulat-beg-oldi-actual-control.*

34. France 24, July 10, 2009, available from *www.france24. com/en/20090710-turkish-pm-erdogan-xinjiang-violence-genocide-turkey-uighurs-han-trade-beijing-china*; and *Today's Zaman*, April 17, 2013, available from *www.todayszaman.com/news-312876-lavrov-slams-friends-of-syria-lays-bare-differences-with-turkey.html*.

35. "*Turtsiya namerena vstupit v ShOS*" ("Turkey Intends to Join the SCO"), *Regnum.ru*, January 26, 2013, available from *www. regnum.ru/news/1617665.html#ixzz2Sdltmnx1*.

36. "*O mezhmidovskikh konsultatsiyakh po dalneyshemu razvitiyu svyazey ShOS s mezhdunarodnymi organizatsiyami*" ("On Inter-MFA Consultations about Further Development of SCO Links with International Organizations"), SCO website, April 10 2013, available from *www.sectsco.org/RU123/show.asp?id=594*.

37. "Is the SCO a threat to Japan?" *Japan Reference*, December 22, 2008, available from *www.jref.com/forum/japanese-news-hot-topics-4/sco-threat-japan-40754/#.UeWF7oxIupo*; Gene Germanovich, "The Shanghai Cooperation Organization: A Threat to American Interest in Central Asia," *China and Eurasia Forum Quarterly*, Vol. 6, No. 1, 2008, pp. 19-38, available from *www.scribd.com/doc/26087287/A-Threat-to-American-Interest-in-Central-Asia*.

38. D. Rogozin, *Yastreby Mira. Dnevnik Russkogo Posla* (*Hawks of Peace: Diary of a Russian Ambassador*), London, UK: Glagoslav Publications Ltd., 2010, pp. 241, 243.

39. According to the Russian state statistics service, the population of the Far Eastern Federal District of the Russian Federation was 6,251,496 people at the beginning of January 2013.

40. Aleksandr Babakin, "На Дальнем Востоке пока все спокойно" ("So Far Everything is Calm in the Far East"), *Nezavisimoye Voyennoye Obozreniye*, June 10, 2005, available from *nvo.ng.ru/wars/2005-06-10/2_fareast.html*.

41. Sergey Kazennov and Vladimir Kumachev, "Не надо абсолютизировать "угрозу с Востока" ("The Threat from the East Should Not be Taken in Absolute Terms"), *Nezavisimoye Voyennoye Obozreniye*, August 13, 2010, available from *nvo.ng.ru/concepts/2010-08-13/12_menace.html*.

42. Aleksandr Sharavin, "Третья угроза" ("The Third Threat"), *Nezavisimoye Voyennoye Obozreniye*, September 28, 2001, available from *nvo.ng.ru/wars/2001-09-28/5_danger.html*.

43. Keir Giles, "The Military Doctrine of the Russian Federation 2010," Rome, Italy: NATO Defense College, February 2010, available from *www.academia.edu/343489/The_Military_Doctrine_ of_the_Russian_Federation_2010*; Keir Giles, "Russia's National Security Strategy to 2020," Rome, Italy: NATO Defense College, June 2009, available from *www.academia.edu/343512/Russias_ National_Security_Strategy_to_2020*.

44. Russian military doctrine accepts the use of nuclear weapons when the enemy uses weapons of mass destruction or threatens the very existence of the state.

45. Igor Korotchenko, "Военный экспорт Поднебесной как вызов для отечественного ОПК" ("China's Military Exports as a Challenge to the Domestic Defense Industry"), *Nezavisimoye Voyennoye Obozreniye*, October 29, 2010, available from *nvo.ng.ru/ armament/2010-10-29/10_china.html*.

46. The organization evolved into an intergovernmental military alliance after the signing of the Collective Security Treaty (CST) in May 1992 by Russia, Armenia, Belarus, Kazakhstan, Kyrgyzstan, and Tajikistan. Uzbekistan joined as a full member in 2006, but suspended its membership as it was unhappy with Moscow's dominance of the organization.

47. Konstantin Parshin, "Uzbekistan and Tajikistan: Souring Political Relations Damaging Human Ties," *Eurasianet.org*, October 3, 2012, available from *www.eurasianet.org/node/65994*; Shavkat Kasymov, "Dammed or Damned: Tajikistan and Uzbekistan Wrestle Over Water-Energy Nexus," *World Policy Blog*, April 2, 2013, available from *www.worldpolicy.org/blog/2013/04/02/ dammed-or-damned-tajikistan-and-uzbekistan-wrestle-over-water- energy-nexus*; "Uzbekistan 'cuts off gas' to Tajikistan," *The Australian*, January 1, 2013, available from *www.theaustralian.com.au/ news/breaking-news/uzbekistan-cuts-off-gas-to-tajikistan/story-fn3dx- ix6-1226545967186*.

48. See "U.S. Relations With Tajikistan," Washington, DC: U.S. Department of State, November 16, 2012, available from *www.state.gov/r/pa/ei/bgn/5775.htm*.

49. Viktoriya Panfilova, "Душанбе заигрывает с Вашингтоном" ("Dushanbe Flirts With Washington"), *Nezavisimaya Gazeta*, February 20, 2013, available from *www.ng.ru/cis/2013-02-20/7_tadjikistan.html*.

50. Vladimir Mukhin, "Tsentral'noaziatskii mirotvorcheskii vopros," *Nezavisimaya Gazeta*, February 20, 2013, p. 7.

51. "Backgrounder: U.S. Military Bases in Central Asia," New York: Council for Foreign Relations, available from *www.cfr.org/russia-and-central-asia/asia-us-military-bases-central-asia/p8440*. See also "How the Andijan killings unfolded," BBC News, May 17, 2005, available from *news.bbc.co.uk/1/hi/4550845.stm*.

52. Panfilova.

53. See, for example, Raffi Khatchadourian, "US Eyes Bases in Tajikistan," *Eurasianet*, November 4, 2001, available from *www.eurasianet.org/departments/insight/articles/eav110501a.shtml*.

54. Joshua Kucera, "Why is Tajikistan's Ayni Air Base Idle?" *Eurasianet*, July 9, 2010, available from *www.eurasianet.org/node/61503?quicktabs_11=2*.

55. "*Informatsionnoye soobshcheniye po itogam zasedaniya Soveta glav gosudarstv-chlenov ShOS*" ("Information issued after the meeting of the Council of Heads of States which are Members of the SCO"), Russian presidential website, June 7, 2012, available from *xn--d1abbgf6aiiy.xn--p1ai/%D1%81%D0%BF%D1%80%D0%B0%D0%B2%D0%BA%D0%B8/1233*.

56. Russian MFA website, in English, June 6, 2005, as reported by BBC Monitoring Service; item subsequently removed from Russian MFA website.

57. "Shanghai to Host Sixth SCO Summit this June," UzReport Information Agency, January 17, 2006, available from *mir.uzreport.uz/news_e_6721.html*.

58. Website of Russian Embassy in Beijing, available from *www.russia.org.cn/rus/2887/31292107*. Also see "О ратификации Соглашения о банке данных Региональной антитеррористической структуры Шанхайской организации сотрудничества." Закон Республики Казахстан от 22 мая 2006 года N 142. ("On the Ratification of the Agreement on the Data Bank of the Regional Antiterrorist Structure of the Shanghai Cooperation Organisation." Law of the Republic of Kazakhstan of May 22, 2006, N 142), available from *agentura.ru/infrastructure/sharing/rats/bd/*; and Ведомости Парламента Республики Казахстан, 2006 г., N 9, ст. 50; "Казахстанская правда" от 25 мая 2006 года N 127-128 (25098-25099) (Bulletin of the Parliament of the Republic of Kazakhstan, 2006, N 9, Art. 50"; "Kazakhstan Pravda" on May 25, 2006, N 127-128 (25098-25099).

59. "SCO Culture Ministers gather in Beijing," SCO website, June 7, 2012, available from *www.sectsco.org/EN123/show.asp?id=335*.

60. "Charter of the Shanghai Cooperation Organization," June 7, 2002, as published in *China Daily*, June 12, 2006, available from *www.chinadaily.com.cn/china/2006-06/12/content_6020341.htm*.

61. *Ibid*.

62. Confidential interviews with author, 2006.

63. "History of development of SCO," *Window of China*, August 21, 2008, available from *news.xinhuanet.com/english/2008-08/21/content_9572869.htm*.

64. *Istoriya RATS* (*The History of the RATS*), RATS website, June 17, 2006, available from *ecrats.org/en/about/history/*.

65. "Regionalnaya antiterroristicheskaya struktura (RATS) ShOS" ("The Regional Anti-Terrorist Structure (RATS) of the SCO"), *Agentura.ru*, available from *www.agentura.ru/infrastructure/sharing/rats/*.

66. *Novoye Pokoleniye*, in Russian, September 3, 2004. Kasymov's criticism of the CSTO was subsequently confirmed to the

author by several officials from SCO countries. The heads of the SCO member states issued a declaration on August 28, 2008, calling for strengthening of SCO cooperation with the CIS and the CSTO, and follow-up memoranda signed in March 2009 facilitated working meetings of the SCO with members of the secretariat of the CSTO and the anti-terrorist centre of the CIS. *Infoshosru,* April 29, 2009, available from *www.infoshos.ru/ru/?idn=4120.*

67. Viktoriya Panfilova, "Bednost kak osnova terrorizma" ("Poverty as the Root of terrorism"), *Nezavisimaya Gazeta,* February 7, 2005, available from *www.ng.ru/dipkurer/2005-02-07/11_poverty.html.*

68. The Regional Anti-Terrorist Structure (RATS) of the SCO.

69. Panfilova.

With the help of the RATS, the Kazakhstan security service dismantled the 'Dzhamoat' organization which trained its members for suicide actions against the embassies of the USA, Israel, and the office of the Uzbek general prosecutor. The Uzbek branch of the same organisation was eliminated when it tried to set up a bomb factory near Bukhara. The sect 'Akramya' in the Uzbek Andijan was also dismantled as was another group, 'Bayat' in Tajikistan.

70. Vyacheslav Kasymov, "S 'chernym internatsinalom' v belykk perchatkakh ne boryutsya" ("The Black International Cannot be Fought in White Gloves"), *Vesti.uz,* June 20, 2006, available from *www.vesti.uz/index.php?option=com_content&view=article& id=22802:2006-06-20+00:00:00&catid=19:politics&Itemid=39.*

71. "Antiterroristicheskaya struktura ShOS sodeystvovala arestu bole 400 terroristov" ("The Anti-Terrorist Structure of the SCO Facilitated the arrest of More than 400 Terrorists"), *Avesta.tj,* June 21, 2012, available from *www.avesta.tj/security/12813-antiterroristicheskaya-struktura-shos-sodeystvovala-arestu-bolee-400-terroristov.html.*

72. *O podpisanii soglasheniya o banke dannykh RATS SCO (On the Signing of an Agreement on the SCO RATS Database), Aly-ans* Media, available from *www.allmedia.ru/laws/DocumShow.*

asp?DocumID=91179; "Decree of 24 July 2004 #310 On Signing the Agreement on the Database of the Regional Anti-Terrorist Structure of the Shanghai Cooperation Organization," available from *www.hrichina.org/content/5224.*

73. *Doklad Soveta RATS ShOS Sovetu glav gosudarstv-chlenov ShOS o deyatelnosti RATS ShOS v 2004 godu* ("Report by the SCO RATS Council to the Council of SCO Heads of State on the Activity of the SCO RATS in 2004"), Russian MFA website, July 5, 2005, available from *www.mid.ru/ns-rasia.nsf/3a0108443c964002432569e7 004199c0/432569d80021985fc32570350039ead2.*

74. "'1mn Died' from Afghan Heroin, Drug Production '40 Times Higher' since NATO Op," *Russia Today,* April 3, 2013, available from *rt.com/news/afghanistan-heroin-production-increased-266/.*

75. "*Itogi IV Soveshchaniya rukovoditeley kompetentnykh organov gosudarstv-chlenov ShOS, nadelennykh polnomochiyami po borbe so nezakonnym oborotom narkotikov*" (*"Results of the IV Meeting of SCO Member States' Heads of Organs Empowered to Combat Drug Trafficking"*), April 30, 2013, available from *www.sectsco.org/RU123/show. asp?id=613.*

76. "*Na perednem kraye borby s 'tremya salami zla'*" ("At the forefront of the fight against the 'three evil forces'"), *Infoshos,* April 29, 2009, available from *www.infoshos.ru/ru/?idn=4120/.*

77. "Predstaviteli ShOS dogovorilis o protivodeystvii verbovke v terroristicheskiye organizatsii" ("SCO Representatives Agree to Counteract Recruitment Into Terrorist Organisations"), *Mir Islama,* April 1, 2013, available from *www.mirislama.com/ news/5276-predstaviteli-shos-dogovorilis-o-protivodeystvii-verbovke-v-terroristicheskie-organizacii.html;* "В Ташкенте прошло очередное заседание Совета РАТС ШОС" ("A Regular Meeting of the SCO RATS Council Took Place in Tashkent"), *Avesta.Tj,* April 1, 2013, available from *www.avesta.tj/security/17588-v-tashkente-proshlo-ocherednoe-zasedanie-soveta-rats-shos.html.*

78. "O zasedanii Soveta natsionalnykh koordinatorov ShOS" ("On the meeting of the Council of National Coordinators of SCO"), April 12, 2013, available from *www.sectsco.org/RU123/ show.asp?id=599.*

79. "China's New Leadership Supports Security Cooperation within SCO: Official," *Xinhuanet*, April 29, 2013, available from *news.xinhuanet.com/english/china/2013-04/29/c_132349531.htm*.

80. "Shankhayskaya organizatsiya sotrudnichestva" ("Shanghai Cooperation Organisation"), *Newsruss.ru*, available from *newsruss.ru/doc/index.php/%D0%A8%D0%B0%D0%BD%D1%85 %D0%B0%D0%B9%D1%81%D0%BA%D0%B0%D1%8F_%D0% BE%D1%80%D0%B3%D0%B0%D0%BD%D0%B8%D0%B7%D0 %B0%D1%86%D0%B8%D1%8F_%D1%81%D0%BE%D1%82% D1%80%D1%83%D0%B4%D0%BD%D0%B8%D1%87%D0%B5 %D1%81%D1%82%D0%B2%D0%B0*.

81. Aleksander Lukin, "The Shanghai Cooperation Organization: What Next?" *Russia in Global Affairs*, August 8, 2007, available from *eng.globalaffairs.ru/number/n_9132*.

82. Artur Fazleev, "Бюджет саммита ШОС в Уфе поделят два бюджета и инвесторы" ("The Budget of the SCO Summit in Ufa Will be Shared by Two Budgets and Investors"), *Kommersant. ru.*, February 5, 2013, available from *kommersant.ru/doc/2120808*. The budget for the SCO meeting in Ufa may also cover a meeting of BRIC countries also scheduled to take place there.

83. According to Transparency International, Kazakhstan is 133rd on the list, available from *www.transparency.org/country#KAZ*; Tajikistan, 157th, available from *www.transparency.org/country#TJK*; and Uzbekistan 170th, available from *www.transparency.org/country#UZB*.

84. "Stronger Economic Cooperation Highlighted at SCO Forum," *Xinhuanet*, April 18, 2013, available from *news.xinhuanet.com/english/china/2013-04/18/c_132322780.htm*.

85. Lukin.

86. "РФ выступила против длительного иностранного присутствия в Афганистане" ("Russia Opposes a Long-term Foreign Presence in Afghanistan"), *RIA Novosti*, December 18, 2012, available from *ria.ru/world/20121218/915200816-print.html*.

87. Kasymov.

88. For more detail, see "Russia: Future Directions," Shriven-ham, Swindon, Wiltshire, UK: Advanced Research and Assess-ment Group, Defence Academy of the UK, October 1, 2008.

APPENDIX I

THE SCO TODAY

The Council of Heads of Government.

The supreme decisionmaking body of the Shanghai Cooperation Organization (SCO) is the Council of Heads of State (HSC), responsible for defining strategic priorities of the organization and mapping out its actions. Each member state presides for 1 year, and the year ends with a SCO summit when another country takes over. The annual meetings of the HSC allow the heads of states to make decisions and give instructions on all major issues concerning the SCO activities.

HGC approves the SCO budget and decides the main economic issues relevant to the SCO activities. The HGC also meets once every year to discuss a strategy for multilateral cooperation, concentrating mainly on economic issues and on adopting the SCO budget.

The Council of Foreign Ministers.

The Council of Foreign Ministers monitors and guides the current activities of the SCO, and conducts consultations within the SCO foreign relations remits. The council is empowered to issue statements on behalf of the SCO.

Minister and heads of the national agencies of the SCO member states occasionally meet to address specific issues concerning the organization. Such meetings are determined by the Council of Heads of State and the Council of Heads of Government. The SCO has also the Council of National Coordinators which coordinates the current activities of the organization such as meetings of Speakers of Parliament, Secretaries of Security Councils, Foreign Ministers, Ministers of Defense, Emergency Relief, Economy, Transportation, Culture, Education, Healthcare, Heads of the Law Enforcement Agencies, Supreme Courts, Courts of Arbitration, and Prosecutors General. The Council of National Coordinators is staffed by some of the most experienced and competent officials representing the member states.

The SCO Secretariat.

The Secretariat is the main permanent executive body of the organization. It is based in Beijing, China, and provides organizational and technical support for activities of the SCO and drafts annual budget proposals. The Secretary General is appointed for 3 years by the Heads of State Council.[1] The Secretary General is also in charge of the SCO Business Council which has its secretariat in Moscow, Russia.

The Secretariat:

1. Coordinates and provides informational, analytical, legal, organizational, and technical support for the activities of the organization, in conjunction with the SCO Regional Anti-Terrorist Structure (RATS). It formulates the proposals concerning the development of cooperation within the SCO framework and external ties of the organization, and oversees the fulfillment of decisions adopted by the SCO bodies.

2. Together with the national Permanent Representatives, composes draft documents based on the proposals of the member states and, with the consent of the Council of National Coordinators, circulates them among the member states for further consideration by the SCO institutions, including draft agendas of the

forthcoming meetings of the SCO institutions, as well as necessary materials, and agrees on the dates and venues of these meetings. Materials and documents mentioned in the given paragraph are forwarded to the member states not later than 20 days before the start of these meetings.

3. Together with the Council of National Coordinators, arranges consultations of experts of the member states and drafts documents submitted to meetings of the SCO institutions.

4. Provides the organizational and technical support for meetings of the SCO institutions, in accordance with the relevant regulations, and cooperates with states hosting such meetings.

5. Carries out the duty of a depositary of documents, certifies, and forwards to the member states copies of such documents, as well as to the SCO RATS, when appropriate. Certified copies of documents adopted by the SCO are handed out to Permanent Representatives within 7 days after the Secretariat has received original documents.

6. Prepares and publishes information catalogues, manages the website of the Secretariat, and coordinates its contents with that of the website of the SCO RATS and the SCO Regional Economic Cooperation website. Holds regular briefings for representatives of the media.

7. Carries out preliminary legal and financial assessment of draft treaties and regulations drawn up in the SCO framework.

8. In conjunction with the SCO, RATS composes a general plan of the organization's activities for the following 6 months.

9. Has the right to request the member states to provide reference books and other open source materials for working needs of the SCO institutions.

10. Ensures protocol support of the Secretary General's activity.

11. Together with the SCO RATS, maintains contacts with states and international organizations and, with the consent of the member states, prepares appropriate documents for such contacts.

12. With the consent of the Council of National Coordinators, and working with the SCO RATS, coordinates the organization's cooperation with observers and dialogue partners, in accordance with the legal rules of the SCO.

13. Works with nongovernmental structures in the SCO, in accordance with the SCO's legal rules and regulations.

14. With the consent of the member states and within budgetary limits, recruits experts on the basis of a single term contract for conducting research on issues of specific concern to the SCO. He/she also organizes workshops and conferences.

15. Arranges and coordinates the activities of the SCO Observer Mission, in accordance with the regulations on SCO Observer Mission in presidential and/or parliamentary elections, as well as referendums.[2]

The Secretariat and the RATS are the only two permanently functioning bodies of the SCO, but in contrast with the RATS, the SCO Secretariat is only a supporting administrative organ with very limited decisionmaking powers.

ENDNOTES - APPENDIX I

1. "Shanghai Cooperation Organisation," Ministry of Foreign Affairs of Belarus website, available from *www.mfa.gov.by/en/organizations/membership/list/c2ee3a2ec2158899.html*. "Brief introduction to the Shanghai Cooperation Organisation," SCO website, available from *www.sectsco.org/EN123/brief.asp*.

2. "SCO Secretariat in Brief," SCO website, available from *www.sectsco.org/EN123/secretariat.asp*.

APPENDIX II

KEY IMPLEMENTERS:
THE GENERAL SECRETARIES
AND THE EXECUTIVE DIRECTORS

The two most significant positions in the Shanghai Cooperation Organisation (SCO) are those of the SCO Secretary General and the Regional Anti-Terrorist Structure (RATS) Executive Director (for this reason, biographies of the individuals who have held these posts are provided in the succeeding pages.) Until recently, the first was expected to be a seasoned diplomat with a good knowledge of his own diplomatic service, foreign language abilities, and extensive foreign diplomatic experience, which would allow them to interact with the SCO member states, with members of international organizations, and with Beijing-based foreign ambassadors and other officials. The RATS Executive Directors, meanwhile, had to be experienced security managers. In both cases, these are the two highest ranking national officials. They are expected to run the international organizations, but also monitor events as the representatives of their own states at the same time.

The SCO's first Secretary General, Chinese diplomat Zhang Deguang, had impeccable credentials. A graduate in Russian literature from the Beijing Institute of Foreign Languages, he served as Deputy Minister of Foreign Affairs and on diplomatic postings in Washington and as Chinese ambassador to Russia. He took up his post at the SCO on January 1, 2004, and was replaced 3 years later by Bolat Nurgaliyev who graduated in the 1970s from the Foreign Language Faculty of the Tselinograd State Pedagogical

Institute and later from the Komitet Gosudarstvennoy Bezopasnosti (Russian Secret Police, better known as the KGB) Intelligence School. Nurgaliyev served as a Soviet intelligence officer under diplomatic cover in Pakistan between 1981 and 1985, and in India between 1990 and 1992. In 1992, Nurgaliyev joined the Kazakh Ministry of Foreign Affairs and between 1994 and 1996 was Deputy Minister of Foreign Affairs of Kazakhstan. In January 2007, before he became the SCO Secretary General, he was the Kazakh ambassador to the United States, South Korea, and Japan. On January 1, 2010, he was replaced by Muratbek Sansyzbayevich Imanaliyev, a qualified historian of the Far East and Chinese translator who was previously the Kyrgyz ambassador to China, twice Kyrgyz Minister of Foreign Affairs (1991-92 and 1997-2002), a politician, and a Professor at the American University of Central Asia.

The latest incumbent, Dmitry Fedorovich Mezentsev from Russia, is different than his predecessors. He has enjoyed an illustrious career, but his arrival with the SCO raised eyebrows, when in 2006 he came straight from the position of Deputy Chairman of the Federation Council of the Russian Federal Assembly to the SCO Business Council, which he left in 2009 to return to Russian administration as Governor of Irkutsk Region. Since 2008, he also has been the Head of the Political Psychology Department of the Saint Petersburg University. In effect, he is the least qualified Secretary General to date.

The reason for this may lie in Mezentsev's early career. A graduate of the Leningrad Railway Transport Engineering Institute, Mezentsev became an activist in the Soviet All-Union Leninist Young Communist League (Komsomol) and between 1984 and 1990 was a Political Officer in the Soviet Army. In 1990, Mezentsev became a People's Deputy of Leningrad City Council, and between 1991 and 1996 was Chairman of the Media Committee of the Saint Petersburg city administration, where he worked with both Vladimir Putin and Dmitry Medvedev. When their common political boss and mayor of St. Petersburg, Anatoliy Sobchak, lost the 1996 election, both Putin and Mezentsev moved to Moscow, where Putin worked in the Presidential Administration and Mezentsev became Deputy Chairman of the Russian Federation State Press Committee. Three years later, Dmitry Mezentsev was President of the Centre of Strategic Research, both, one of the principal information providers for Putin's presidential election campaign in 2000, and a strategic planning center for Putin's subsequent agenda such as the Strategy for the Socio-Economic Development of the Russian Federation to 2010. Here, he worked alongside other senior Russian figures such as German Gref and Elvira Nabiullina. By proposing Mezentsev for Secretary General, Putin installed a loyal associate rather than the man most qualified to lead the organization in its own interests. In addition, Putin also has a direct representative at the SCO, the experienced and knowledgeable diplomat Kirill Barsky, appointed in 2011 as the Russian national coordinator in the SCO and later promoted to Russian presidential envoy.

If it is desirable for the SCO's general secretaries to have some diplomatic or international experience, then professional competence and experience is absolutely essential for Executive Secretaries of the RATS. The first Executive Secretary, Major General Vyacheslav Temirovich Kasymov, started his career in the Soviet KGB and, after 1991, continued in the Uzbek National Security Service, becoming Deputy Chairman of the organization. His replacement, Colonel General

Myrzakan Usurkanovich Subanov, took over in January 2007. A professional Soviet army officer, Subanov was the first Defence Minister of Kyrgyzstan. Before joining the SCO, he was the Chairman of the Kyrgyz Border Guard Service. He was replaced in 2010 by Dzhenisbek Mukhamedkarimovich Dzhumanbekov, Deputy Chairman of the Kazakh State Security Committee (KNB), who started his professional career in 1972 in the Union of Soviet Socialist Republics (USSR) KGB and, in 1992, moved to the KNB where he held several high-level positions, including as the KNB's official representative in Russia and Uzbekistan.

The latest Executive Secretary of RATS, Zhang Xinfeng, is a professional security officer. He held several important positions in China's Public Security regional departments, and in 2003 was transferred to Beijing, to the Ministry of Public Security (MPS). In 2005, Zhang Xinfeng became Deputy Director of the National Narcotics Control Commission, Deputy Director of the People's Armed Police Force, and Deputy Public Security Minister. Without losing any of these positions, in 2011, he was appointed Deputy Director of the State Internet Information Office. Zhang Xinfeng is expected to work in this position until the end of 2015. His nomination shows that Beijing treats RATS appointments seriously.

SCO General Secretaries.

Zhang Deguang
Born in February 1941 in the Shandong province.
1965 -   Graduated from the Beijing Institute of Foreign Languages, in Russian literature, and joined the Ministry of Foreign Affairs (MFA).

1965 - 1973	Translator in the Chinese MFA.
1973 - 1977	Attaché at the Chinese Embassy in Moscow.
1977 - 1987	Second Secretary, First Secretary, Deputy Director of the Chinese – Russian Negotiations Department of the USSR and European Affairs at the Chinese MFA.
1987 - 1992	Counsellor at the Chinese Embassy in Washington.
1992 - 1993	Ambassador Extraordinary and Plenipotentiary to Kazakhstan.
1993 - 1995	Head of the Department of Eastern Europe and Central Asia, at the Chinese MFA.
1995 - 2001	Deputy Minister of Foreign Affairs.
2001 - 2003	Ambassador to Russia.
In May 2003,	Zhang Deguang was appointed Secretary General of the Secretariat of the SCO. He took up his post on January 1, 2004.[1]

Bolat Kabdylkhamintuly Nurgaliyev

Born in Blagodatnoye village, Aqmola District (Kazakhstan) in July 1951.

1972 -	Graduated from the Foreign Languages Faculty of the S. Seifulin Tselinograd State Pedagogical Institute and later from the Red Banner KGB Institute. (Intelligence)
1972 - 1973	Lecturer at the Tselinograd Pedagogical Institute.
1973 - 1980	Unspecified position in the Soviet Ministry of Defence.
1981 - 1985	Attaché, Third Secretary at the USSR Embassy in Pakistan.

1985 - 1990	Second and then First Secretary of the USSR MFA.
1990 - 1992	First Secretary of the Soviet Embassy in India.
1992 - 1994	Counsellor, head of the International Security and Armaments Control Directorate of the Kazakh MFA.
1994 - 1996	Deputy Minister of Foreign Affairs of Kazakhstan.
1996 - 2000	Kazakh Ambassador to the USA, Canada and Mexico.
2000 - 2003	Kazakh Ambassador to South Korea.
2003 - 2006	Kazakh Ambassador to Japan.
2007 - 2009	Secretary General of the SCO.
2010 - (January 1)	Special Representative of the OSCE Chairman.
2012 - (April)	Kazakh Ambassador to Israel and, since November 2012, also to Cyprus.[2]

Muratbek Sansyzbayevich Imanaliyev
Born: February 1956 in Bishkek (Kyrgyzstan).

1978 -	Graduated from the Institute of Africa and Asia of the Moscow State University, with a degree in history of the Far East and as a Chinese translator.
1982 -	Postgraduate studies at the Leningrad Eastern Studies Institute of the USSR Academy of Science.
1982 - 1991	Second Secretary, Head of a department and acting Deputy Minister at the Kyrgyz SSR MFA.
1991 - 1992	Minister of Foreign Affairs of the Kyrgyz Republic.
1993 - 1996	Kyrgyz Ambassador in China.

1996 - 1997	In charge of the Foreign Affairs Department of the president of Kyrgyzstan.
1997 - 2002	Minister of Foreign Affairs of Kyrgyzstan.
2002 - 2007	Professor at the American University of Central Asia.
2004 -	Became a cofounder of the JanyBagyt (New Course) movement.
2005 - 2009	President of the Public Policy Institute.
2009 - (January)	Advisor to the President of the Kyrgyz Republic.
2010 - (January 1)	Secretary General of the SCO.[3]

According to unconfirmed information, between 1992 and 1993, Imanaliyev was Councilor at the Russian Embassy in China.

Dmitry Fedorovich Mezentsev
Born in Leningrad in August 1959.

1981 -	Graduated the Leningrad Railway Transport Engineering Institute. Foreman at the Leningrad-Baltiysk locomotive depot.
1983 - 1984	Communist Youth Movement activist in Leningrad.
1984 - 1990	Officer in the printing media of the Soviet Army.
1990 - 1991	People's Deputy of the Leningrad City Council, in charge of the Press Centre of the Leningrad City Council.
1991 - 1996	Chairman of the Media Committee of the St. Petersburg Town Hall and Publishing and Media Committee, representative of the Information and Press Ministry of the Russian Federation.

1996 - 1999	Deputy Chairman of the Russian Federation State Press Committee.
1999 - 2003	President of the Centre of Strategic Research in Moscow.
2002 - 2009	Representative of the Irkutsk Region Administration at the Council of Federation of the Federal Assembly of the Russian Federation, Chairman of the Information Policy Committee.
2004 - 2009	Deputy Chairman of the Council of Federation of the Federal Assembly of the Russian Federation
2006 -	Appointed Special Representative on SCO Business Council affairs.
2009 -	Re-elected SCO Business Council Chairman.
2009 - 2012 -	Governor, Chairman of the Government of Irkutsk Region.
Since 2008 -	Head of the Political Psychology Department of St. Petersburg State University, Ph.D. in political psychology, doctoral candidate of Moscow State Institute (University) of International Relations. Decorations: "Order of Merit to the Motherland Fourth Degree," Order of Honour, medals, officer of the National Order of the French Legion of Honour, medal "For the strengthening of Russo-Chinese friendship."[4]
2013 -	Secretary-General of Shanghai Cooperation Organization. On June 7, 2012, appointed (January 1, 2013, through December 31, 2015). Ambassador-at-large of the Russian Federation Ministry of Foreign Affairs

RATS Executive Directors.

Vyacheslav Temirovich Kasymov (2004-07)
Major General
Born in 1948 in Bukhara region.
Graduated from the Tashkent Institute of Irrigation
and Agricultural Mechanisation Engineering
1980 - 1991   Served in the KGB USSR.
1991 - 1996   Head of a Directorate of the Uzbek Na-
              tional Security Service (SNB).
1996 -   Deputy Chairman of the SNB.
2004 - 2007   Appointed as First Executive Director of
              the RATS of the SCO.

Myrzakan Usurkanovich Subanov (2007-09)
Colonel General
Born in October 1944, in Tash Tube (Kyrgyzstan).
1966   Graduated from the Tashkent Higher
              Combined Arms School.
1977   Graduated from the Frunze Military
              Academy.
1984   Graduated from the USSR General Staff
              Academy.   Commanded the 1st Mo-
              torised Rifle Division in Kaliningrad.
1987 - 1989   Adviser to the Afghan Ministry of De-
              fence.
1989 - 1991   Commander of an army corps in the
              Leningrad Military District.
1991 -   First Deputy Commander and the Chief
              of Staff of the Turkestan Military Dis-
              trict.
1992 -   First Deputy Chairman, then Chairman,
              of the Kyrgyz State Defence Committee.
1993 - 1999   Defence Minister of Kyrgyzstan.

| 2005 - 2006 | Chairman of the Kyrgyz Border guard Service. |
| 2007 - 2009 | Executive Director of RATS. |

Dzhenisbek Mukhamedkarimovich Dzhumanbekov (2010-13)
Lieutenant General
Born in November 1945.

1968 -	Graduated from the Moscow Technological Institute of the Food Industry and worked in the Kazakh SSR Ministry of Bread Production [sic] in Almaty.
1972 -	Graduated from an unspecified KGB school and worked as a KGB officer in Almaty and Karaganda regions.
1986 -	Deputy Head of the Kazakh KGB, of the KGB USSR, of the Aktyubinsk region.
1992 -	Head of the Kazakh KGB/KNB of the Dzhambyl region.
1994 -	First Deputy of the Chairman of the Kazakh National Security Committee (KNB).
1995 - 1997	Chairman of the National Security Committee of Kazakhstan.
1997 -	Deputy Director of Barlay/Intelligence Service of the Kazakhstan
1999 - 2002	Official KNB Representative in Uzbekistan.
1992 - 2004	Official KNB Representative in Russia.
2004 - 2009	Deputy Director of the Executive Committee of the RATS of the SCO.
2009 -	Deputy Chairman of the Kazakh KNB.
2010 - 2013	Executive Director of the RATS.

Zhang Xinfeng (2013 -)
Born in 1952 in Tieling City in Liaoning Province.
His working career - probably in the state security sector - began in 1968, a year before the official end of the Cultural Revolution, and joined the Communist Party of China in 1976, the year Mao Zedong died.

1980 - 1983	Worked for the Public Security Department, Culture Protection Division, Heilongjiang Province.
1983 - 1984	Deputy Director, Public Security Department, Criminal Investigation Division Heilongjiang Province
1984 -1990	Director of the Public Security Department, Criminal Investigation Division in Heilongjiang Province.
1995 - 2003	Deputy Director, then Director of the Public Security Department, Heilongjiang Province, Promoted to Director, Ministry of Public Security, Criminal Investigation Department.
2003 - 2005	Assistant Minister, Ministry of Public Security.
2005 -	Deputy Director, National Narcotics Control Commission.
	Deputy Director, Chinese People's Armed Police Force.
	Deputy Director, National Narcotics Control Commission.
	Member of the CPC Party committee at Ministry of Public Security CPC.
	Deputy Minister of Public Security Ministry.
2012 - (April)	Deputy Director, State Internet Information Office.

ENDNOTES - APPENDIX II

1. *Peoples.ru,* available from *www.peoples.ru/state/ politics/chzhan_deguan/;* SCO website at *www.sectsco.org/home. asp?LanguageID=2.*

2. "Kazakh News," *Kazinform,* July 4, 2012, available from *www.knews.kg/ru/people/454/print/;* "New Secretary-General of the SCO Muratbek Imanaliev Officially Took Office," *Infoshos,* undated, available from *infoshos.ru/en/?idn=5353;* "About the Embassy, Ambassador," Kazakh Embassy in Israel, undated available from *www.kazakhemb.org.il/?CategoryID=162&ArticleID=734&Page=1.*

3. "Imanliev Muratbek Sansyzbayevich," Knews, July 21, 2013, available from *www.knews.kg/ru/people/454/* and *aef.kz/ ru/aef2011/speakers/61019/;* "Imanliev Muratbek Sansyzbayevich," *Central Asia.ru,* available from *www.centrasia.ru/person2. php?&st=1013869298.*

4. "Secretary-General, Dmitry Federovich Mezentsev," SCO website, available from *www.sectsco.org/EN123/secretary.asp.*

www.ingramcontent.com/pod-product-compliance
Lightning Source LLC
Chambersburg PA
CBHW072016290526
45787CB00013B/921